Household Uses for
Baking Soda

Over 100
Helpful Solutions & Tips

ARM & HAMMER
THE STANDARD OF PURITY

One Box, Countless Uses.

pil

Publications International, Ltd.

Louis Weber, CEO
Publications International, Ltd.
7373 North Cicero Avenue
Lincolnwood, IL 60712

Permission is never granted for commercial purposes.

ISBN-13: 978-1-4508-0109-6
ISBN-10: 1-4508-0109-9

Manufactured in China.

8 7 6 5 4 3 2 1

Publications
International, Ltd.

Contents

Baking Soda Basics

Put over 160 years of versatility and value to work throughout your home.

Now, the cleaning and freshening secret that has been passed down for generations is yours. There's almost nothing ARM & HAMMER® Baking Soda can't do. You can trust its natural, pure, and gentle power to tackle jobs in every room of your home— and beyond! ARM & HAMMER® Baking Soda is strong enough to lift away dirt, but still gentle and non-abrasive on delicate surfaces. And when it comes to odors, ARM & HAMMER® Baking Soda

neutralizes and eliminates them at the source.

Try these effective, money-saving solutions and make the secret of ARM & HAMMER® Baking Soda yours today!

Baking Soda Basics

The tips you'll find in this book use ARM & HAMMER® Baking Soda in four different ways: Directly, in a solution, as a paste, and as an additive. Follow these guidelines for each use when a specific measurement isn't given. For added convenience, ARM & HAMMER® Baking Soda is available in an array of sizes and forms, making choosing the right product for any job easy.

1. Use Directly

Baking Soda is sprinkled directly on the surface or onto a sponge for use. It is not diluted.

2. Make a Solution

Use 4 tablespoons of Baking Soda for each quart of warm water.

3. Make a Paste

Add just enough water to the Baking Soda to achieve a consistency that will not run if applied to a vertical surface.

4. As an Additive

Follow the directions for each tip, adding the appropriate amount of Baking Soda to improve the cleaning and deodorizing performance of products you already use in your home.

Chapter 1

Personal Care

When you're making time to take care of you, ARM & HAMMER® Baking Soda has easy and affordable ways to help you refresh and relax. Baking Soda is the simple, all-natural secret to glowing skin; softer, more manageable hair; fresher breath; and so much more.

Refreshing Bath Soak

Taking a bath is so last year…until now! Add ½ cup of ARM & HAMMER® Baking Soda to your bath for a relaxing and refreshing soak. Your skin will feel silky smooth, and it's a great way to get away from it all.

Brightening Manicure

Dip brush into ARM & HAMMER® Baking Soda and scrub nails and cuticles. Make a paste of 3 parts ARM & HAMMER® Baking Soda to 1 part water. Rub in a gentle, circular motion over hands and fingers to exfoliate and smooth. Rinse clean with warm water and apply polish as usual.

Brushes and Combs

For lustrous hair with more shine, keep brushes and combs clean. Remove natural oil build-up and hair product residue by soaking combs and brushes in a solution of 1 teaspoon of ARM & HAMMER® Baking Soda in a small basin of warm water. Rinse and allow to dry.

Antacid

Spicy food is yummy until it bothers the tummy. ARM & HAMMER® Baking Soda is a safe and effective antacid to relieve heartburn, sour stomach, and/or acid  indigestion, when used as directed. Always refer to the ARM & HAMMER® Baking Soda package for instructions.*

Directions:
Add ½ teaspoon to ½ glass (4 ounces) of water every 2 hours, or as directed by a physician. Dissolve completely in water. Accurately measure ½ teaspoon.**

*Warnings:
• Ask a doctor before use if you have a sodium restricted diet.
• Ask a doctor or a pharmacist before use if you are taking a prescription drug. Antacids may interact with certain prescription drugs.
• Do not administer to children under age 5.
• STOMACH WARNING: TO AVOID SERIOUS INJURY, DO NOT TAKE UNTIL POWDER IS COMPLETELY DISSOLVED. IT IS VERY IMPORTANT NOT TO TAKE THIS PRODUCT WHEN OVERLY FULL FROM FOOD OR DRINK. Consult a doctor if severe stomach pain occurs after taking this product.
• Stop use and ask a doctor if symptoms last more than 2 weeks.
**Do not take more than the following amounts in 24 hours:
• Seven ½ teaspoons
• Three ½ teaspoons if you are over 60 years.
Do not use the maximum dosage for more than 2 weeks.

Other Information:
Each ½ teaspoon contains 616 g sodium.
Refer to the ARM & HAMMER® Baking Soda package for detailed instructions before using.

Hand Cleanser

Give yourself a hand with
ARM & HAMMER® Baking Soda.
Forget the harsh soaps and gently
scrub away ground-in dirt and
neutralize odors on hands
with a paste of 3 parts
ARM & HAMMER®
Baking Soda to 1
part water, or add 3
parts ARM & HAMMER®
Baking Soda to your liquid
hand soap. Then rinse clean.
Your skin will feel softer too!

Mouth Freshening

Bad breath keeping you
tight-lipped? Open up for
ARM & HAMMER® Baking
Soda. Put 1 teaspoon
in half a glass of water,
swish, spit, and rinse.
(Avoid swallowing excess
rinse solution.) Odors
are neutralized—not just
covered up—so get ready
to pucker up!

Foot Soak

Here's a great way to start your home pedicure. Dissolve 3 tablespoons of ARM & HAMMER® Baking Soda in a basin of warm water and soak feet. Gently scrub with a paste of ARM & HAMMER® Baking Soda. The hardest part is deciding which color nail polish you'll use this week!

Mouth Cleansing

Clean up your mouth! Use ARM & HAMMER® Baking Soda to help keep teeth clean and white! Sprinkle some ARM & HAMMER® Baking Soda in a small dish, dip in your damp toothbrush, brush, and rinse throroughly to freshen those pearly whites.*

ARM & HAMMER® Baking Soda does not contain the anti-cavity ingredient fluoride. Use it where water is fluorinated or when a non-fluoride toothpaste is desired for adult use or as directed by your dentist or physician.

Hair Care

For locks that rock, remember to shake it. Sprinkle a small amount (quarter-size) of ARM & HAMMER® Baking Soda into your palm along with your favorite shampoo. Shampoo as usual and rinse thoroughly. (Be careful to avoid eye area when rinsing.) The ARM & HAMMER® Baking Soda helps remove the residue that styling products leave behind so your hair is cleaner and more manageable.

Smelly Sneakers

Smelly sneakers are embarrassing and completely preventable. Simply shake a little ARM & HAMMER® Baking Soda into them between wearings. It works by absorbing odor-causing moisture while neutralizing existing odors. Use at least once a week or more if you wear the shoes frequently. Tap out excess Baking Soda before wearing your sneakers again.

Oral Appliance Soak

Soak oral appliances like retainers, mouthpieces, and dentures in a solution of 2 teaspoons ARM & HAMMER® Baking Soda dissolved in a glass or small bowl of warm water. Then rinse throroughly. The ARM & HAMMER® Baking Soda loosens food particles and neutralizes odors to keep appliances fresh! You can also brush appliances clean using ARM & HAMMER® Baking Soda.

Plaque

Tooth decay may result from food debris that leads to plaque build-up. ARM & HAMMER® toothpastes, with the power of Baking Soda, penetrate deep down into the crevices between your teeth and gums to remove plaque in hard-to-reach places.

Deodorant

A quick pit stop. Dust ARM & HAMMER® Baking Soda under arms as needed to feel fresh all day. The magic of ARM & HAMMER® Baking Soda naturally absorbs odors instead of just covering them up.

Bug Bites Be Gone

Baking Soda temporarily protects and helps relieve minor skin irritation and itching due to insect bites. Refer to the ARM & HAMMER® Baking Soda package for detailed instructions before using.*

Facial and Body Exfoliator

Are you a fan of the self-tan? Before applying products that give you a glow, give yourself an invigorating, yet gentle, facial and body scrub with ARM & HAMMER® Baking Soda. Removing dead skin cells will leave your skin soft and smooth, perfect before application. Make a paste of 3 parts ARM & HAMMER® Baking Soda to 1 part water. Rub in a gentle circular motion to exfoliate the skin. Rinse clean, being careful to avoid eye area.

Shaving

Men with sensitive skin
may find that a solution of
1 tablespoon ARM & HAMMER® Baking Soda in
1 cup water makes a great preshave treatment or a
soothing aftershave treatment. Avoid eye area.

Razor Burn

For instant relief of razor burn, dab on an
ARM & HAMMER® Baking Soda solution.

Sunburn Pain

For sunburn pain, saturate a washcloth with a solution of
4 tablespoons ARM & HAMMER® Baking Soda in
1 quart water. Apply to affected area.

Poison Ivy, Oak, and Sumac Irritation

Ease irritation from poison ivy, oak, and sumac. Refer
to the ARM & HAMMER® Baking Soda package
for detailed instructions before using. *

*Warnings:
• When using this product, do not get into eyes.
• In some cases, soaking too long may overdry.
• Stop use and ask a doctor if conditions worsen or symptoms last more
than 7 days or clear up and occur again within a few days.

Directions:
For adults and children 2 years of age and older, children under 2 years
ask a doctor.

For a paste: add enough water to the Baking Soda to form paste. Apply
to the affected area of skin as needed or as directed by a doctor.

For a soak in the bath: dissolve 1 to 2 cups in a tub of warm water. Soak
for 10 to 30 minutes or as directed by doctor. Pat dry (do not rub) to
keep a thin layer on the skin.

For use as a compress or wet dressing: add Baking Soda to water to
make a mixture in a container. Soak a clean, wet cloth in the mixture.
Apply cloth loosely to affected area for 15 to 30 minutes. Repeat as
needed or directed by a doctor. Discard mixture after each use.

Chapter 2

Baby & Nursery Care

We have a special place in our hearts and a long history of caring for families, and lots of ways to help! All-natural ARM & HAMMER® Baking Soda is a pure and gentle choice to safely clean and freshen baby's home environment. From deodorizing baby bottles to neutralizing diaper odors, trust ARM & HAMMER®.

Freshen Stuffed Animals

Even Mr. Bear needs a freshening. Keep favorite cuddly toys fresh with a dry shower of ARM & HAMMER® Baking Soda. Just sprinkle ARM & HAMMER® Baking Soda on dry toys and let it sit for 15 minutes before thoroughly brushing off to remove residue. It's gentle enough for use around your baby and Teddy will appreciate it too!

Deodorize Baby Bottles

Do you know what goes in your baby's mouth? For safe cleaning and deodorizing, fill bottles with warm water and add 1 teaspoon of ARM & HAMMER® Baking Soda. Shake, rinse, and thoroughly clean as usual. For extra cleaning and deodorizing, you can also soak bottles and nipples overnight in a solution of 4 tablespoons of ARM & HAMMER® Baking Soda to 1 quart of warm water. Then rinse and clean as usual.

Cleaning Baby Equipment

Little hands mean lots of exploring. Safely clean your baby's area (play pen, changing table, crib, stroller, car seat, and high chair) with ARM & HAMMER® Baking Soda. Just sprinkle ARM & HAMMER® Baking Soda directly on a clean, damp sponge and rub the item clean. Wipe down thoroughly and allow to dry. Sparkling clean and no harsh cleaners to worry about!

Baby Spills on Carpet

Even little ones can make big messes! Clean and deodorize baby spills or accidents on carpets by soaking up as much of the spill as possible. Clean the stain according to the carpet manufacturer's directions and allow to dry. Then, to deodorize, when the area is completely dry, sprinkle liberally with ARM & HAMMER® Baking Soda and let sit for 15 minutes before vacuuming it up. Check for color-fastness first before applying ARM & HAMMER® Baking Soda.*

Deodorize Diaper Pails

Whoa! A smell this powerful needs to be neutralized. Sprinkle ARM & HAMMER® Baking Soda liberally over dirty disposable diapers in the diaper pail.

Make Bath Water Soothing

Add ¼ cup of ARM & HAMMER® Baking Soda to a regular tub, or a few tablespoons to a baby tub, with warm water for a soothing soak for baby's bottom and skin.

CAUTION: Before use, test hidden area of carpet for color-fastness. Mix ½ tablespoon in ½ cup water and pour small amount on carpet. Let dry, vacuum, and check carpet.

Baby Laundry

ARM & HAMMER® Baking Soda is gentle enough for even the tiniest baby clothes, yet effective enough for big baby odors. For tough stains, add ½ cup of ARM & HAMMER® Baking Soda with your liquid laundry detergent, or a ½ cup in the rinse cycle for deodorization!

Clean Baby Combs

Harsh chemicals are a hair-raising thought. Keep baby combs and brushes clean by soaking them in gentle solution of 1 teaspoon of ARM & HAMMER® Baking Soda in a small basin of warm water. Rinse and allow to dry.

Cleaning Baby Toys

Don't toy around with harsh cleaners. Clean and deodorize baby toys safely and effectively using 4 tablespoons of ARM & HAMMER® Baking Soda dissolved in 1 quart of warm water. Wash toys with a clean, damp sponge or cloth, rinse, and dry.

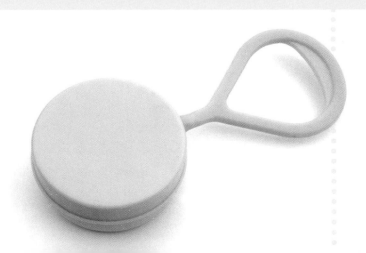

Chapter 3

Fun for Kids

Who doesn't love easy and fun ideas to entertain kids and help them learn, all for about a dollar a solution? ARM & HAMMER® can help with great Baking Soda projects and crafts, like safe, non-toxic Play Clay™ and our famous Erupting Volcano. We have great ways to play!

Water Colors

Have an urge to create? These paints mix up in minutes with items you have in your kitchen! Experiment to get the most vibrant colors for your masterpiece. (Do not eat or drink the watercolors. Children should use only under adult supervision.)

WHAT YOU NEED:
- 2 tablespoons ARM & HAMMER® Baking Soda
- 2 tablespoons flour
- 2 teaspoons sugar
- 1 packet* dry unsweetened drink mix (any flavor)
- 2 tablespoons water

HOW TO MAKE IT:
1. Mix dry ingredients in a bowl.
2. Add water and stir until fizzing stops. (Different flavors of the drink mix will yield different colors.)
3. For more intense watercolor, a few drops of food coloring can be added to the mix.
4. Paint with them right away, or pour into jars with lids and try to let harden for future use.

*Packets vary in size, depending on flavor. Use enough drink mix to make 2 quarts. Remember the importance of adult supervision, especially with young children.

Sneaker Peekers

This fun craft does double duty. Kids will have a blast decorating these zany creatures—and then the ARM & HAMMER® Baking Soda will go to work deodorizing those smelly sneakers!

WHAT YOU NEED:

- Newspaper
- 1 new, white athletic sock (mid-calf size)
- 1 cup ARM & HAMMER® Baking Soda
- 1 rubber band
- 6-inch ribbon or string
- Felt, markers, buttons, and glue for decorating!

HOW TO MAKE IT:

1. Lay newspaper down on your work surface.

2. Fill the sock with 1 cup ARM & HAMMER® Baking Soda.

3. Secure with rubber band.

4. Tie ribbon around rubber band, cut off extra sock (cuff area).

5. Decorate! Use felt, markers, buttons, sequins, etc. to make your sneaker peeker an animal, a monster, or a flower! Anything goes!

6. Double the supplies to make two peekers to stick in your sneakers overnight for fresh shoes in the morning! (Remember the importance of adult supervision, especially with young children.)

Erupting Volcano

This is an old favorite that's a staple at science fairs. (Be sure to supervise young children.)

WHAT YOU NEED:
- Cardboard
- 3 (4 ounce) plastic cups
- Plaster-of-Paris
- ¼ cup vinegar
- Few drops of hand dishwashing liquid
- Few drops of water
- Few drops of red food coloring
- 1 teaspoon ARM & HAMMER® Baking Soda

HOW TO MAKE IT:

1. On baking sheet (or other easily cleaned surface), shape cardboard into broad cone shape using a cup to form a "crater" at the top of the volcano.

2. Use Plaster-of-Paris over the cone to form the volcano (do not get plaster into the crater). Allow volcano to dry completely.

3. Paint or decorate volcano as desired.

4. Mix vinegar with dishwashing liquid, water, and red food coloring in a plastic cup.

5. Put ARM & HAMMER® Baking Soda into a small, empty plastic cup. Place this cup inside the volcano crater.

6. Quickly pour vinegar mixture into the ARM & HAMMER® Baking Soda cup in the crater. Enjoy the "lava" as the volcano erupts!

EXPLANATION:

The ARM & HAMMER® Baking Soda reacts with the vinegar in the mixture and produces a gas: carbon dioxide (CO^2). The gas releases bubbles through the dishwashing liquid and food coloring, creating the bubbly, red lava.

Cork Races

Use the reaction between ARM & HAMMER® Baking Soda and vinegar to create a racing game!

WHAT YOU NEED:
- Tape
- Several lengths of clear plastic tubing (1 inch inner diameter, each approximately 3 feet in length)
- 1 tablespoon ARM & HAMMER® Baking Soda
- Painted cork balls (¾ inch diameter or small enough to pass easily through tubing)
- ½ cup vinegar
- Hand dishwashing liquid
- Small container with spout

HOW TO MAKE IT:
1. Tape up 1 end of each tube to be the bottom.
2. Stand tubes upright on a flat surface (baking sheet or tray) and pour ARM & HAMMER® Baking Soda into the bottom.
3. Drop a cork ball into each tube.
4. Make a mixture of vinegar and dishwashing liquid in the spouted container.
5. Pour the mix carefully down the inside of the tube and watch the cork ride the suds to the top. Keep face away from top of tube to avoid being splashed. (Supervise use with young children.)

EXPLANATION:
The Baking Soda reacts with the vinegar in the mixture and produces a gas: carbon dioxide (CO_2). As the gas

is released it bubbles through the dishwashing liquid, creating the suds that push the cork to the top.

VARIATIONS:

- Experiment with different mixes of vinegar, ARM & HAMMER® Baking Soda, and dishwashing liquid and have races to find the mix that makes the fastest cork.

- Mark the tubes ⅔ of the way to the top. Experiment with mixes and quantities to get the cork to stop closest to the mark.

- Try ping-pong balls instead of cork balls and use wider-diameter tubing.

Footprints

Let the kids have some holiday fun while you clean and eliminate odors! Sprinkle some ARM & HAMMER® Baking Soda in a stencil to leave Santa footprints on the rug. When the kids are done playing (or after 15 minutes), vacuum the Baking Soda to freshen carpets.*

*CAUTION: Before use, test hidden area of carpet for color-fastness. Mix ½ tablespoon in ½ cup water and pour small amount on carpet. Let dry, vacuum, and check carpet.

Play Clay™

Play Clay™ is homemade modeling clay that hardens after drying. Three simple ingredients combine for virtually unlimited creative possibilities for kids of all ages. Play Clay™ is great for rainy days, birthday parties, and class activities. Use it to make decorations, ornaments, jewelry, magnets, boxes, and more!

WHAT YOU NEED:
- 2 cups ARM & HAMMER® Baking Soda
- 1 cup cornstarch
- 1¼ cups cold water (can add food coloring to color clay)

HOW TO MAKE IT:
1. Stir together ARM & HAMMER® Baking Soda and cornstarch in saucepan.

2. Add water (and food coloring, if desired) and cook over medium heat, stirring constantly, until mixture reaches consistency of moist mashed potatoes (approximately 10 to 15 minutes).

3. Remove mixture to plate and cover with a damp cloth.

When Play Clay™ is cool to the touch, pat until smooth. Now you're ready to make fun shapes! (Do not eat clay. Children should use with adult supervision.) Once done playing, air dry clay shapes on a wire rack (8 hours or overnight). Or, preheat oven to lowest setting. Turn off, then place finished shapes on a cookie sheet in oven for 10 to 15 minutes. Decorate with paint, markers, or glitter, or add your favorite objects (like buttons and shells) with a small amount of glue. Store any unused Play Clay™ in the refrigerator for up to 1 week (store in a tightly sealed plastic bag or container). Do not freeze.

Play Clay™ Hanger
Capture a child's handprint in Play Clay™ by pressing into damp clay. When dry, paint and add the child's name and date on back, then attach a picture hanger.

Play Clay™ Frame
Cut a square or rectangle from Play Clay™ then cut a frame opening the size of a favorite photograph. Leave a ½-inch border. Use another piece of clay for a stand to attach to the back. Decorate the frame.

Play Clay™ Plaques

Create a name plaque for a child's room by cutting out the shapes of letters and attaching them to a rectangular piece of Play Clay™ as the background. Paint and finish when dry.

Play Clay™ Jewelry

Shape beads for a necklace by rolling Play Clay™ into oval or round shapes. Press a toothpick through to make holes for stringing.

Play Clay™ Threading

String Play Clay™ beads on thread, shoelaces, yarn, kite string, or fishing line. Tie knots between beads to hold them in place.

Play Clay™ Earrings

To make earrings or a brooch, create small shapes with a flat backside and glue to earrings or pin backings.

Play Clay™ Napkin Rings

Make fancy napkin rings by rolling out a long, narrow rectangle of clay, then piecing the ends together into a ring.

Play Clay™ Ornaments

Use cookie cutters to make tree ornaments. While the ornament is still wet, make a hole near the top for hanging. Add an ornament hook or ribbon to hang the ornament.

Play Clay™ Paintings

Paint dry pieces with watercolor, poster, or acrylic paints. Draw with a felt-tip pen or waterproof marker. Apply glitter to wet paint.

Tips for Working with Play Clay™

1. Smooth rough or cracked edges of Play Clay™ with an emery board.

2. Finish Play Clay™ objects with a clear acrylic spray or clear nail polish.

Inflate a Balloon

Remove the cap sealing ring from an empty 2-liter soda bottle. Pour 1 cup of vinegar into the bottle. Prestretch your balloon and fill with 2 tablespoons of ARM & HAMMER® Baking Soda. Close the neck of the balloon with a bobby pin, leaving enough room at the end of the balloon to stretch over the bottle's neck. Carefully place balloon over neck of bottle and down about ¾ of an inch so the ring of the balloon is sealed around the neck. Remove the bobby pin and invert the balloon to dispense Baking Soda into the bottle. To remove: gently raise the edge of the balloon to allow the gas to escape in a direction away from you.

Chapter 4

Cleaning & Freshening Homes with Pets

Pets bring lots of love into a home, but you don't have to live with their odors! You can use the power of ARM & HAMMER® Baking Soda to eliminate even the toughest pet odors, from litter boxes to carpets and upholstery and more.

Dirty Dog

Use ARM & HAMMER® Baking Soda to give your dog a dry bath. Start when your dog's coat is thoroughly dry. Give fur a light sprinkle of ARM & HAMMER® Baking Soda, use a brush to work it through, and then thoroughly remove. It's an easy way to freshen your best friend's coat in between baths.

Cat Litter Deodorizer

Cat got your nose? ARM & HAMMER® Baking Soda freshens your cat's litter box for oh so 'pawfect' freshness. Cover the bottom of the pan with ARM & HAMMER® Baking Soda, then fill as usual with litter. To freshen between changes, sprinkle ARM & HAMMER® Baking Soda on top of the litter after a thorough cleaning. For even stronger litter box deodorization, try ARM & HAMMER® Cat Litter Deodorizer specially formulated to effectively destroy cat litter box odors on contact. Keeps any litter smelling fresher, longer.

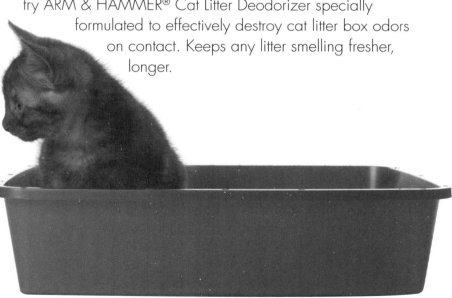

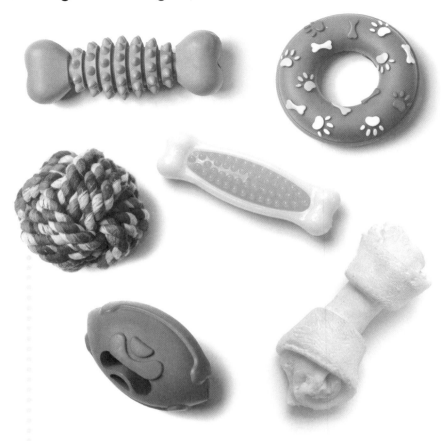

Dirty Pet Toys

Don't play catch with chemicals. Clean plastic and rubber toys safely by washing in a solution of ARM & HAMMER® Baking Soda (4 tablespoons dissolved in 1 quart of warm water). Give furry toys a dry shower by sprinkling ARM & HAMMER® Baking Soda on dry toys, and brushing off to thoroughly remove ARM & HAMMER® Baking Soda after 15 minutes.

Litter Box Odor

Litter box odor can spoil an otherwise clean, fresh home. Keep it under control with ARM & HAMMER® Cat Litter. Your family (and your cats) will thank you. Try ARM & HAMMER® Multi-Cat Extra Strength Clumping Litter for households with more than one cat. ARM & HAMMER® Essential® Natural Clumping Litter has virtually no dust and is made of natural corn fibers.

Freshen Pet Bedding

You love your pets, but you don't have to live with their odors. Eliminate odors from your pet's bedding by sprinkling liberally with ARM & HAMMER® Baking Soda, then wait 15 minutes (longer for stronger odors) and vacuum up thoroughly.*

*CAUTION: Before use, test hidden area of bedding for color-fastness. Mix ½ tablespoon in ½ cup water and pour small amount on bedding. Let dry, vacuum, and check bedding.

Chapter 5

Bathroom Cleaning & Freshening

ARM & HAMMER® Baking Soda is the safe, effective way to leave your whole bathroom sparkling clean and smelling fresh, without the need for harsh chemicals. You can even use ARM & HAMMER® Baking Soda on high-gloss surfaces like fiberglass and tiles without worrying about scratches!

Surface-Safe Cleaning

Glub in the tub? For safe, effective cleaning of bathroom tubs, tile, and sinks—even shiny fiberglass and glossy tiles— sprinkle ARM & HAMMER® Baking Soda lightly on a clean damp sponge and scrub as usual. Rinse thoroughly and wipe dry. Afterwards, take a nice relaxing bath.

Deodorizing Wastebasket

Defeating odors in the bathroom often feels like a waste of time. Keep bathroom wastebaskets fresh-smelling with just a sprinkle of ARM & HAMMER® Baking Soda. Apply regularly as you add to the container, or when you empty it, wash the container with a solution of 1 cup of ARM & HAMMER® Baking Soda per 1 gallon of water.

Septic Care

Regular use of ARM & HAMMER® Baking Soda in your drains can help keep your septic system flowing freely. We recommend adding 1 cup of ARM & HAMMER® Baking Soda per week to help maintain a favorable pH in your septic tank.

Shower Curtains

Clean and deodorize your vinyl shower curtain by sprinkling ARM & HAMMER® Baking Soda directly on a clean, damp sponge or brush. Scrub the shower curtain and rinse clean. Hang it up to dry.

Deodorizing Drains

What goes down sometimes comes back up. To deodorize your sink and tub drains, and keep lingering odors from resurfacing, pour ARM & HAMMER® Baking Soda down the drain (½ cup) while running warm tap water. ARM & HAMMER® Baking Soda will neutralize both acid and basic odors for a fresh drain. Here's a tidbit to remember: When replacing your box of ARM & HAMMER® Baking Soda Fridge-n-Freezer® Odor Absorber (every 30 days), pour the contents of the old box down the drain to get a little extra mileage.

Cleaning Bathroom Floors

Leave it up to ARM & HAMMER® Baking Soda to speed things up in the bathroom. ARM & HAMMER® Baking Soda helps remove the dirt and grime from bathroom tiles or no-wax floors quickly and easily. Mix ½ cup ARM & HAMMER® Baking Soda in a bucket of warm water, mop, and rinse clean for a sparkling floor.

Chapter 6

Laundry, Carpets, Floors & Household Use

No other product does more throughout your home than ARM & HAMMER® Baking Soda, so think outside of the box to help boost the cleaning and freshening power of your laundry detergent and remove crayon marks from walls. With so many solutions, there's almost nothing ARM & HAMMER® Baking Soda can't do!

Laundry Booster

Give your laundry a boost—then give yourself a hand! Add ½ cup of ARM & HAMMER® Baking Soda to your laundry to make liquid detergent work harder for you and your family. A better balance of pH in the wash gets clothes cleaner, fresher, brighter! Our large size resealable pouch size makes it an easy additive for every wash load.

Cleaning Furniture

Being sent to your room never looked so good. Clean and remove marks (even crayon!) from walls and painted furniture by applying ARM & HAMMER® Baking Soda to a damp sponge and rubbing lightly. Wipe off with a clean, dry cloth.

Carpet Odors

Sprinkle ARM & HAMMER® Baking Soda directly on carpets and wait 15 minutes before vacuuming thoroughly. You'll freshen your carpets while eliminating household odors.*

*CAUTION: Before use, test hidden area of carpet for color-fastness. Mix ½ tablespoon in ½ cup water and pour small amount on carpet. Let dry, vacuum, and check carpet.

Freshen Sheets

Get towels and linens clothesline fresh—right from the wash! Add ½ cup of ARM & HAMMER® Baking Soda to the rinse cycle and get ready for the great outdoors.

Freshen Closets

Just like the refrigerator, your closets can collect stale smells. So the ARM & HAMMER® Baking Soda Fridge-n-Freezer® Odor Absorber box does double duty here too! Place a box on the shelf to keep the closet smelling fresh. Remember to replace it every 30 days for optimal freshness!

Musty Towels

Fun in the sun can
make towels smell musty.
Get pool towels
clothesline fresh—right
from the wash! Add ½ cup
ARM & HAMMER® Baking
Soda to the rinse cycle.

Laundry Stains

Tough laundry stains need a
tough laundry solution. Remove strong dirt and stains
like blood, grass, and sauce with ARM & HAMMER®
Plus OxiClean® Laundry Detergent. ARM & HAMMER®
Plus OxiClean® Laundry Detergent combines OxiClean®
stain removers with the cleaning and
freshening power of ARM & HAMMER®
Baking Soda.

Cleaning Floors

With all the pitter-patter of little feet in the kitchen, your floor is bound to get dirty. Remove dirt and grime (without unwanted scratch marks!) from no-wax and tile floors using ½ cup ARM & HAMMER® Baking Soda in a bucket of warm water; mop and rinse clean for a sparkling floor. For unsightly scuff marks, use ARM & HAMMER® Baking Soda on a clean, damp sponge, then rinse. Great for high-traffic areas and after dinner parties too!

Clean and Freshen Sports Gear

Be a good sport. Use an ARM & HAMMER® Baking Soda solution (4 tablespoons ARM & HAMMER® Baking Soda in 1 quart warm water) to clean and deodorize smelly sports equipment like fishing and camping gear. Sprinkle ARM & HAMMER® Baking Soda into golf bags and gym bags to deodorize and—abbra caddabra—the odors are gone! Clean golf irons (without scratching them!) with an ARM & HAMMER® Baking Soda paste (3 parts ARM & HAMMER® Baking Soda to 1 part water) and a brush. Rinse thoroughly and let dry.

Deodorize Gym Bags

Put an ARM & HAMMER® Baking Soda Fridge-n-Freezer® Odor Absorber box in your gym locker—and another in your gym bag! The removable front and back flaps let air flow through the box without messy spills!

Upholstery Spills

Pet accidents, kid accidents, even adult accidents—clean spills or accidents on upholstery by soaking up as much of the liquid as possible. Clean the stain according to the manufacturer's directions and allow to dry. Then to deodorize, when the area is completely dry, sprinkle with ARM & HAMMER® Baking Soda and let sit for 15 minutes before vacuuming it up. Check for color-fastness first before applying ARM & HAMMER® Baking Soda.*

*CAUTION: Before use, test hidden area of upholstery for color-fastness. Mix ½ tablespoon in ½ cup water and pour small amount on upholstery. Let dry, vacuum, and check upholstery.

Freshen Ashtrays

Cover up smells by sprinkling
ARM & HAMMER® Baking
Soda in the bottom of ashtrays.
Replace the Baking Soda
when you empty the ashtray.
As an added bonus, the
ARM & HAMMER® Baking Soda helps extinguish
cigarettes and cigars!

Freshen Upholstery

Something neat for your seat! Keep comfy upholstered
sofas and chairs smelling fresh with ARM & HAMMER®
Baking Soda. Sprinkle Baking Soda on upholstery, wait
15 minutes, and vacuum up.*

*CAUTION: Before use, test hidden area of upholstery for color-fastness.
Mix ½ tablespoon in ½ cup water and pour small amount on upholstery.
Let dry, vacuum, and check upholstery.*

Allergens

Stale air can be unpleasant and unhealthy. ARM & HAMMER® Air Filters in your home's heating & cooling system neutralize common household odors and capture airborne allergens, viruses, and more.

Deodorize Garbage Can

A couple of shakes is all it takes! Keep unpleasant smells to a minimum by sprinkling ARM & HAMMER® Baking Soda in the garbage between layers as they accumulate. Periodically wash out and deodorize garbage cans with a solution of 1 cup of ARM & HAMMER® Baking Soda per 1 gallon of water.

Recyclables

Keep those recyclables smelling fresh until collection day. Sprinkle ARM & HAMMER® Baking Soda on top as you add to the container.

Also, clean your recyclable container periodically by sprinkling ARM & HAMMER® Baking Soda on a damp sponge. Wipe clean and rinse.

Silver Tarnish Remover

Place a sheet of aluminum foil in the bottom of a baking pan. Sprinkle 1 to 2 teaspoons of ARM & HAMMER® Baking Soda and ½ teaspoon of salt on the foil. Add about 5 cups of boiling water to the pan to dissolve the ARM & HAMMER® Baking Soda and salt. Carefully (water will be very hot) place the tarnished silverware in the solution, making sure the silverware touches the aluminum foil. Let it stand for 2 to 3 minutes and carefully remove. Rinse the silverware well, and then use a soft cloth to buff dry. (We recommend polishing after tarnish removal to protect your silverware for future use.)

Flower Vases

To clean glass vases you've used for your beautiful flowers, fill three-quarters full with hot water, add a teaspoon of ARM & HAMMER® Baking Soda, and shake. Let sit, then rinse.

Fireplaces

Clean smoky buildup from your glass fireplace or wood-burning stove or oven. Crumple a piece of newspaper, wet it with water, and sprinkle some ARM & HAMMER® Baking Soda on it. Rub the dirty area of the glass and wipe it down with a damp, clean cloth. The residue will come off without scratching the glass.

Chapter 7

Kitchen & Cooking

ARM & HAMMER® Baking Soda goes way beyond freshening the fridge and freezer—it's the original kitchen multi-tasker. It can help you safely clean fruits and vegetables for your favorite meals, and then make washing pots and pans easier by lifting away baked-on food. It is the ultimate solution for cleaning stainless surfaces without scratching for a sparkling kitchen. And, ARM & HAMMER® Baking Soda is the secret for delicious baked goodies!

Funky Fridge

A funky fridge can spoil the flavor of your fresh food. Change the ARM & HAMMER® Baking Soda box every 30 days to stop flavor transfer and keep foods tasting fresher, longer. Don't wait until your food tells you, change it today.

Greasy Dishes

Greasy dishes overwhelm even the most effective detergents. To cut through the toughest grease, add 2 heaping tablespoons of ARM & HAMMER® Baking Soda to detergent and dishwater. Let pans soak for 15 minutes, then clean.

Dirty Microwave

Dirty microwaves retain the odor of everything we cook in them. For instant cleaning and deodorizing, sprinkle ARM & HAMMER® Baking Soda on a damp sponge and gently wipe the inside and outside of your microwave. To keep odors at bay, place a box of ARM & HAMMER® Baking Soda Fridge-N-Freezer® Odor Absorber in the microwave between uses—don't forget to replace it every 30 days for maximum freshness.

Dishwashers

Sprinkle ARM & HAMMER® Baking Soda in the bottom of the dishwasher to absorb food odors just lingering in the dishwasher. Double duty! Use ARM & HAMMER® Baking Soda to deodorize before you run the dishwasher.

Tomatoes

Cut the acidic level of tomato sauce or chili by adding a pinch of ARM & HAMMER® Baking Soda.

Coffee Maker

A cleaner coffee maker is a simple soak away. Just add ¼ cup ARM & HAMMER® Baking Soda to 1 quart of warm water to clean coffee makers, mugs, and more. For really tough stains, add dishwasher detergent and soak them in this solution overnight. Then simply sprinkle ARM & HAMMER® Baking Soda on a damp sponge and gently wipe away stains. Rinse thoroughly.

Canning Tips

Clean mineral deposits and neutralize any acids in old canning jars by shaking an ARM & HAMMER® Baking Soda solution inside. Rinse thoroughly, then sterilize as usual.

Clean & Deodorize Lunch Boxes

Keep today's egg salad from tasting like yesterday's tuna. Between uses, place a spill-proof box of ARM & HAMMER® Baking Soda Fridge-N-Freezer® Odor Absorber in everyone's lunch box.

Pots & Pans

Eliminate the heavy burden of scrubbing pots and pans! ARM & HAMMER® Baking Soda penetrates and helps lift off baked-on, dried-on foods. Shake on a generous amount of ARM & HAMMER® Baking Soda, add dish detergent and hot water; let sit for 15 minutes and wash as usual.

Fruit & Vegetable Scrub

An apple a day—cleaned the food-safe way!
ARM & HAMMER® Baking Soda is the food safe way to clean dirt and residue off fresh fruit and vegetables. Just sprinkle a little on a vegetable brush or a clean, damp sponge, scrub, and rinse.

Surface Cleaning

Clean your food prep area with natural, food-safe ARM & HAMMER® Baking Soda instead of harsh cleaners. Sprinkle ARM & HAMMER® Baking Soda onto a clean damp sponge or cloth and wipe clean, rinse thoroughly, then dry. Great for counters, stainless steel sinks, cutting boards, microwaves, plastic containers, lunch boxes, back splashes, oven tops, range hoods, and more!

Sponges

Here's something to soak in! Soak stale-smelling sponges in a strong ARM & HAMMER® Baking Soda solution (4 tablespoons of ARM & HAMMER® Baking Soda dissolved in 1 quart of warm water) to get rid of the mess and bring in the fresh.

Plastic Containers

Keep foods stored in plastic containers from tasting like the last leftovers. Wash the containers in between uses with ARM & HAMMER® Baking Soda sprinkled on a clean, damp sponge. For even tougher odors, just soak items in a solution of 4 tablespoons ARM & HAMMER® Baking Soda dissolved in 1 quart warm water.

Deodorizing Freezers

Fresh is best! To help keep foods tasting like they should, replace your ARM & HAMMER® Baking Soda Fridge-N-Freezer® Odor Absorber every 30 days. The unique flow-thru vents expose twice the amount of Baking Soda to absorb the odors that can make other foods (even ice cubes!) taste funky.

Fluffier Mashed Potatoes

With weather getting cooler, we turn to our favorite comfort foods. Throw a pinch of ARM & HAMMER® Baking Soda into potatoes while mashing to make them fluffier.

Baking

Make sure your baked goods "rise" to the occasion! ARM & HAMMER® Baking Soda is widely used as an agent to promote leavening. As ARM & HAMMER® Baking Soda is heated, it releases carbon dioxide, which causes dough or batter to rise, becoming light and porous. For more than 160 years, great bakers have trusted ARM & HAMMER® Baking Soda because it is made with the highest standards.

Silver Polish

What a bright idea! ARM & HAMMER® Baking Soda can shine all your silver in no time at all. Use a Baking Soda paste made with 3 parts ARM & HAMMER® Baking Soda to 1 part water. Rub onto the silver with a clean cloth or sponge. Rinse thoroughly and dry for shining sterling and silver-plate serving pieces. You'll be polished and ready to go for your next dinner party!

Tea Pots

Here's a quick pick-me-up! Remove tea stains and eliminate bitter off-tastes by washing mugs and tea pots in a solution of ¼ cup ARM & HAMMER® Baking Soda in 1 quart of warm water. For stubborn stains, try soaking overnight in the ARM & HAMMER® Baking Soda solution and detergent or scrubbing with ARM & HAMMER® Baking Soda on a clean, damp sponge.

Clean Mushrooms

Avoid soaking mushrooms when cleaning because they will retain water. Instead, wipe them clean with a damp cloth and just a sprinkle of ARM & HAMMER® Baking Soda.

Prepare Potatoes

Add a sprinkle of ARM & HAMMER® Baking Soda to each potato and then scrub using a brush. Dip in water while scrubbing and towel dry for a dirt-free potato that can be roasted and enjoyed skin-on.

Clean Produce Naturally

To remove dirt, wax, and residue from hard-skinned produce, shake ARM & HAMMER® Baking Soda onto wet produce. Rub and rinse. For soft-skinned or leafy produce, sprinkle Baking Soda in a bowl of water. Add produce, agitate, and rinse.

Chapter 8

The Backyard & Beyond

ARM & HAMMER® Baking Soda is ready for tough jobs—even in the garage and outside your home. Make it a part of your outdoor fun, from quick and easy pool care for a crystal clear pool, to a spotless grill and patio furniture for relaxing. ARM & HAMMER® Baking Soda even helps you clean and freshen inside and outside your car!

Camping Necessity

And you thought the tent was essential. ARM & HAMMER® Baking Soda is a must-have for your next camping trip! One box does so much. It's a dishwasher, pot scrubber, hand cleanser, deodorant, toothpaste, and has tons of other uses.

Grimy Pool Toys

Grimy pool toys can ruin a perfectly beautiful day at the pool. Mix ¼ cup ARM & HAMMER® Baking Soda with 1 quart of warm water. Wipe down toys with the solution and rinse. Smaller items may be soaked first and then rinsed.

Easy Pool Care

Come on in, the water's fine! Improve your pool's clarity with ARM & HAMMER® Baking Soda. It's all about the pH. Dive right into our waterproof and resealable large size bags to keep pool water sparkling. (Follow usage directions printed right on the bag.)

Grungy Grills

Grungy grills aren't a welcome part of any backyard barbecue. Clean them up by sprinkling dry ARM & HAMMER® Baking Soda on a damp brush, scrub as needed, and rinse clean. For tough, greasy stains, scrub with a wire brush and a Baking Soda paste (3 parts Baking Soda to 1 part warm water), and rinse thoroughly.

Lawn Furniture

Get ready for your outdoor oasis! Before you pull out your outdoor patio and pool furniture for the season, give it a thorough cleaning with ARM & HAMMER® Baking Soda. And don't forget to keep outdoor furniture fresh in the off-season too—just sprinkle ARM & HAMMER® Baking Soda underneath cushions or inside the storage bag.

Cleaning Door and Window Screens

Before installing door and window screens you've been storing all winter, give them a quick scrub. Dip a damp wire brush into ARM & HAMMER® Baking Soda and scrub screens clean. Rinse with a sponge or hose.

Oil and Grease Stains

Use ARM & HAMMER® Baking Soda to clean up light-duty oil and grease spills on your garage floor or in your driveway. Sprinkle ARM & HAMMER® Baking Soda on the spot and scrub with a wet brush.

Cleaning Cars

Hit the road with ARM & HAMMER® Baking Soda!
Use ARM & HAMMER® Baking Soda to safely clean
your car lights, chrome, windows, tires, vinyl seats,
and floor mats without worrying about unwanted
scratch marks. Use an ARM & HAMMER® Baking Soda
solution of ¼ cup Baking Soda in 1 quart of warm
water. Apply with a sponge or soft cloth to remove
road grime, tree sap, bugs, and tar. For stubborn
stains, use ARM & HAMMER® Baking Soda sprinkled
on a damp sponge or soft brush.

Cleaning Windshields

After a road trip, remove bugs from your car windshield
by making a paste of ARM & HAMMER® Baking Soda
and water, and applying with a damp, clean cloth.

Deodorizing Cars

Leave car odors in the dust! Odors settle into car
upholstery and carpet, so each time you step in and
sit down, they are released into the air all over again.
Eliminate these odors by sprinkling ARM & HAMMER®
Baking Soda directly on fabric car seats and carpets.

Wait 15 minutes (or longer for strong odors) and vacuum up the odors with the ARM & HAMMER® Baking Soda. Check for color-fastness first before applying ARM & HAMMER® Baking Soda.*

CAUTION: Before use, test hidden area of car seats and carpets for color-fastness. Mix ½ tablespoon in ½ cup water and pour small amount on car seats and carpets. Let dry, vacuum, and check car seats and carpet.

Deodorizing Camper Water Tanks

Freshen your RV water tank periodically by flushing with 1 cup ARM & HAMMER® Baking Soda dissolved in 1 gallon warm water. Drain and flush the tank before refilling (do not use ARM & HAMMER® Baking Soda in your drinking water). The ARM & HAMMER® Baking Soda will eliminate stale odors and help remove mineral build-up that makes water taste off.

Index